UFOs

Brandon Robshaw

Published in association with The Basic Skills Agency

Hodder & Stoughton
A MEMBER OF THE HODDER HEADLINE GROUP

Acknowledgements

Cover: Dale O'Dell/Corbis

Illustrations: Mike Bell

Photos: Mary Evans Picture Library; p 5 Mary Evans/Michael Buhler; p 10 Mary Evans/ Fate Magazine

Orders; please contact Bookpoint Ltd, 130 Milton Park, Abingdon, Oxon OX14 4SB. Telephone: (44) 01235 827720, Fax: (44) 01235 400454. Lines are open from 9.00–6.00, Monday to Saturday, with a 24 hour message answering service. You can also order through our website: www.hodderheadline.co.uk

British Library Cataloguing in Publication Data
A catalogue record for this title is available from the British Library

ISBN 0 340 87693 X

First published 2000
This edition published 2002
Impression number 10 9 8 7 6 5 4 3 2 1
Year   2007 2006 2005 2004 2003 2002

Copyright © 2000 Brandon Robshaw

Typeset by SX Composing DTP, Rayleigh, Essex.
Printed in Great Britain for Hodder and Stoughton Educational, 338 Euston Road, London NW1 3BH, by The Bath Press Ltd, Bath.

Contents

1 Falcon Lake

Steve Michalak could not believe his eyes.
Up in the sky were two bright red lights.
Steve didn't know what they were.
He had never seen anything like them.

It was 20 May 1967.
Steve was out near Falcon Lake in Canada.
He was looking for rocks –
the study of rocks was his hobby.
He had just finished his lunch
when the bright red lights
appeared in the sky.

Steve watched.
The lights got lower.
He could now see that they were
large, cigar-shaped objects.
Suddenly one of the strange craft flew
away. The other landed quite close to Steve.

Steve went up to it.
He thought it was a strange new aircraft.
It gave off waves of heat.
Its colour faded from red to grey.
A door opened in the side.
A bright light shone out.
Steve heard voices from inside,
speaking a strange language.

Steve called out.
The door suddenly closed.
He put his hand on it –
but it was red hot!
His glove caught fire.
At the same time, the craft moved
and sent out a blast of heat.
Steve's shirt caught fire.

He fell back and tore off his burning shirt.
The craft took off
and disappeared behind some trees.

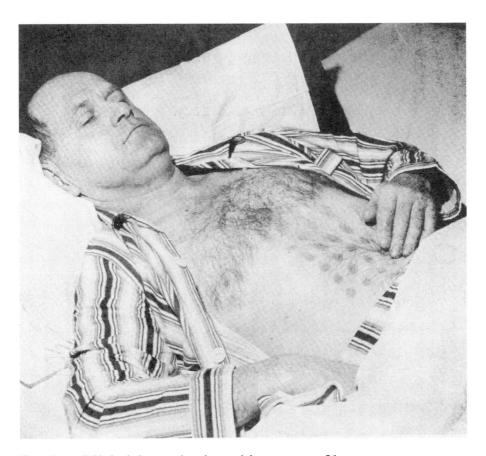

Stephen Michalak received a grid-pattern of burns on
his chest.

Steve felt very sick.
He was in agony from the burns.
He staggered to the road.
A passing motorist picked him up
and took him to hospital.
He was treated for burns.

Steve was ill for a year after this.
He was often sick.
He lost a lot of weight.
He got a strange rash on his chest.
The doctors did not know
what to make of it.

Steve knew it was to do
with the strange craft.
What was it?
Where did it come from?
Was it from Outer Space?

Nobody knows.
Steve had seen – and touched –
a UFO.
An Unidentified Flying Object.

Stephen Michalak approached the door of the UFO.

2 Many Years Ago ...

Stories of UFOs are not new.
The artist Thomas Sandby saw one
over 200 years ago.

It was 18 August 1783.
Thomas was at a party
at Windsor Castle, in Berkshire.
He was out on the terrace
with some other guests.
It was a warm, clear evening.
Suddenly they saw a strange light
up in the sky.

It was round,
about half the size of the moon,
but much brighter.
At first it was pale blue,
then it changed to a bright white light.
It moved very fast through the sky.

It changed its shape and became oblong.
Then it seemed to grow a sort of tail.
It split into two smaller objects –
and it disappeared.

A moment later,
Thomas and the other guests
heard a loud explosion.

Nobody knew what it was.
Scientists said it must have been a meteor
but meteors do not change shape and direction.

Thomas painted a picture of the object.
A copy of his painting
is in the British Museum.
It is the earliest picture we have of a UFO –
before the camera was invented.

3 Flying Saucers

It was 24 June 1947.
Pilot Kenneth Arnold
was flying over the Cascade Mountains
in the USA.
It was a fine, sunny day.

Suddenly, he saw nine strange craft
flying through the sky.
They were like no aircraft
he had ever seen.
They were shaped like boomerangs.
Kenneth guessed they were some new kind
of plane on a test flight.

He guessed they were about twenty miles away.
He thought they must be huge machines
to be visible at that distance.
They were flying much faster than
any plane he had ever seen.
Soon they were out of sight.

Kenneth made a brief stop to re-fuel
in Washington State.
He told some people what he had seen.
Then he took off again for Pendleton, Oregon.

When he landed in Pendleton,
newspaper reporters were waiting for him.
The news had travelled fast.
Everyone wanted to know
about the strange objects he had seen.
The US Air Force did not have any planes
like the ones Kenneth saw.
So what were they?

Kenneth told a reporter
that the craft had moved in a strange way –
'like a saucer would
if you skipped it across water'.
The reporter called the objects
'flying saucers' in his news story.
This was a mistake.
Kenneth did not mean that the objects
were shaped like saucers,
but the name stuck.
Soon, lots of people
were saying they had seen 'flying saucers'.

FATE

SPRING
1948
25¢

THE TRUTH ABOUT
THE FLYING SAUCERS
By KENNETH ARNOLD

MARK TWAIN AND
HALLEY'S COMET
By HAROLD M. SHERMAN

INVISIBLE BEINGS
WALK THE EARTH
By R. J. CRESCENZI

TWENTY MILLION
MANIACS
By G. H. IRWIN

The FLYING DISKS

4 Italy

In the same year, 1947,
there was another report of a UFO.
This one came from Italy.
An Italian writer called Johannis
said he saw a UFO on a river bank.

It was oval-shaped,
red in colour
and about 10 metres wide.
It had no windows.
Two boys were standing beside it.
As Johannis got closer,
he saw that they were not boys.
They were very small adults –
about 90 cm tall.
They had green skin,
big heads and large, staring eyes.

Johannis called and waved at them.
One of them took something from his belt.
He pointed it at Johannis.
There was a puff of smoke
Johannis was knocked flat on his back.
He could not move.

The little green men
got into the craft.
It rose straight up into the sky.

Johannis staggered to his feet.
He went home to bed.

If what Johannis says is true,
the UFO must have come from Outer Space.
The little green men
clearly did not come from Earth.

But is his story true?
Johannis did not publish the story
until years later –
and he was a writer of science fiction.

5 Roswell

There was another strange report from 1947 –
perhaps the most famous UFO story of all.
A UFO is said to have crashed
in the desert in New Mexico.

On 1 July 1947, there was a big storm
in New Mexico. A farmer, William Brazel,
heard a huge explosion.
The next day he rode out on his horse
to see what the damage was.
He found a big hole in the ground,
as if something heavy had crashed there.
Around the hole were pieces of
what looked like tinfoil
and some very tough paper.
The pieces had strange writing on them.
Brazel did not know what they were.
Could they be parts of a flying saucer?

He took the pieces to Roswell Air Force Base.
An officer, Major Marcel, looked at them.
He said the pieces were made of something
very light and thin, but as strong as metal.
He did not know what it was.

The Air Force Base told the papers about it.
Soon, the story was big news.
A flying saucer had crashed!

Soon after this,
Washington got in touch with Roswell Base.
They ordered the officers at Roswell
to say no more about the crash.
They must say that it had been a mistake.
They must say that the pieces
were part of a weather balloon.

The story died down for a while,
but it did not end there.
Another man, Barney Barnett,
said he had seen the crashed UFO.

He also said he had seen the bodies of aliens.
The aliens were small,
with large heads and big eyes.
They had been taken away
to be examined by scientists.
But it was top secret.
The public were told nothing about it.

Later, a film was discovered.
It showed doctors cutting up the
bodies of aliens.
A cameraman said he had
filmed this at Roswell in 1947,
on orders from Washington.
He had kept the film and later sold it.
It was shown on television in 1995.

The film would prove that
an alien space ship crashed that day.
The film would prove that Washington
had covered up the truth.

William Brazel found pieces of what looked like tinfoil and paper on his farm in Roswell, New Mexico.

Was the film real?
Many people think it was a hoax –
just a very clever trick.

What did crash in the desert that day?
Was it a space ship full of aliens?
Or just a weather balloon?

6 Socorro

On 24 April 1964,
another UFO was seen in New Mexico.
Police Officer Zamora was out on patrol
near the town of Socorro.
Suddenly, he heard a loud roar.
He saw a flash of light in the sky.
He drove towards it.
He saw a tall, bright flame
coming down to Earth.
It disappeared behind a hill.

When Zamora got to the top of the hill,
he saw a metal object.
It was about 100 metres away.
It looked like a car standing on one end.
Two children were standing by it.
When Zamora got closer,
they looked more like small men.
They were wearing white suits.

Zamora called the police station.
He said he thought there had been an accident.
He stopped the car.
As he got out, he dropped his radio mike.
He bent to pick it up.

He heard three loud bangs.
Then the roaring noise started again.
He looked up.
He could see now that the metal object
was not a car.
It was shaped like an egg.
It had no doors or windows.
The two small men were gone.
Zamora thought that they must be inside.

The object rose into the air.
A flame roared from underneath it.
It flew off at top speed.

Zamora radioed the police station again.
Other officers came to have a look.
So did scientists.
They found four marks in the sand
where the object had stood.
There were also burn marks nearby.

Other local people said
they had seen the flame
or the egg-shaped craft in the sky.

Nobody ever found out what it was.
This was a clear case of a UFO.
It was an object.
It was flying,
and it was never identified.

7 Iran

On 19 September 1976,
a UFO was seen over Teheran, in Iran.
It was a big white light in the sky,
shining down on the city.

A 23-year-old fighter pilot
named Jafari was sent to investigate.
He flew towards the bright light.
He radioed back to base:
'It's half the size of the moon.
It's violet, orange and white.'

Jafari's plane was a modern jet.
It could fly faster than the speed of sound,
but as he got near,
the UFO shot away.
He tried to catch up with it,
but it moved much too fast.

Then it turned and shot towards him.
Jafari radioed back to base:

'Oh no! It's going to crash into me!'
There was a silence.
Jafari's radio had stopped working.

Then his voice came over again.
'It just missed me!'
Shaken and scared,
Jafari returned to base.

A second plane was sent up
to chase the UFO away.
As it got close,
the UFO shot out a ball of light.
It was coming straight for the fighter plane!
The pilot tried to fire a missile at the UFO.
but nothing happened.
His missiles didn't work.

He dived to avoid the ball of light,
but it followed him.
Just as he thought it must hit him,
the ball of light swerved away.
It went back to the UFO.
It seemed as if the light
had been a warning –
'Don't come too close.'

The UFO then sent out a second ball of light.
This one went straight down.
It lit up the desert near Teheran.
Then the UFO flew away at amazing speed.

The next day the Iranian Air Force
went to took at the desert
where the ball of light had landed.
They found nothing.
People who lived in a farm nearby
said they had seen a blinding light
but there was nothing there now.

The UFO never came back.

8 Attacked!

Bob Taylor was a forester.
He lived in Scotland,
near the town of Livingston.
On the morning of 9 November 1979,
he was walking in the forest with his dog.

As Bob reached a clearing,
he saw a very strange object.
It was a large round ball,
with a ring round it.
It was about the size of a small car.
It hovered just above the ground.
It was grey,
but the colour flickered in a strange way.
One moment it looked solid,
the next moment Bob could see through it.

Bob watched in amazement.
Then two strange things came out.
They were round balls, covered in spikes.
They bounced across the grass towards Bob.

He had no chance to run.
The two things went to each side of him.
There was a strange smell.

Bob felt a burning in his throat.
He felt something pulling at his legs.
Then he fainted.

He woke twenty minutes later.
The strange craft
and the spiky things had gone.
His dog was barking.

Bob got up.
He felt ill.
He tried to drive home,
but crashed the car.
He had to walk home.
When he got home he called a doctor.
The doctor examined him,
but could not say what was wrong with him.

Bob soon felt better.
Shortly after this,
he moved away from the area.
We may never know what attacked him
in the forest that day.

9 Questions

Do UFOs really exist?
The answer is yes.
Every year, all over the world,
people see strange objects in the sky.
Objects which are not identified.

Some of these can be explained.
An Unidentified Flying Object
could be many things:
a comet, a plane, a Frisbee, a balloon.
But not all UFOs can be explained in this way.

Other UFOs could be hoaxes.
Some people enjoy tricking others.
They make up stories just for the fun of it.
But not all UFOs can be explained in this way.
When a UFO is seen by many people,
there must be something there.

Do UFOs come from Outer Space?
We do not know.
The stories about aliens are hard to believe.
There is no real proof.

Would aliens really travel
all this way to visit us
and then not make contact?
Why do they always land
in deserts and forests?
Why not in the middle of London or New York?

We do not know if there are aliens.
But we know that there are UFOs.
One day, we may find out what they are.

This spinning UFO was photographed in California in 1965.